DISCARDED

SPORTS FROM COAST TO COAST™

LACROSSE
RULES, TIPS, STRATEGY, AND SAFETY

CHRIS HAYHURST

rosen central™

The Rosen Publishing Group, Inc.,
New York

Published in 2005 by The Rosen Publishing Group, Inc.
29 East 21st Street, New York, NY 10010

Library of Congress Cataloging-in-Publication Data

Hayhurst, Chris.
Lacrosse: rules, tips, strategy, and safety / by Chris Hayhurst.—1st ed.
    p. cm.—(Sports from coast to coast)
Includes bibliographical references and index.
ISBN 1-4042-0183-1 (library binding)
1. Lacrosse—Juvenile literature. I. Title. II. Series.
GV989.14.H39 2005
796.34'7—dc22

2004000267

Manufactured in the United States of America

CONTENTS

CHAPTER ONE

The History of the Game

Lacrosse combines the best parts of basketball, soccer, and hockey. You don't need to be big and strong to play this game, but you do need to be quick, agile, and coordinated.

You've seen the players running down the field, helmets on, sticks in hand. You've heard them shouting to each other, yelling for the ball. You've seen the moves—the quick stops and starts, the tricky head fakes, the dizzying spins. You've seen this game people call lacrosse. But do you really know what it's all about?

Organized lacrosse has been around for decades. By some accounts, it's the oldest game in North America and has been around for centuries. But it was relatively recently, in the last twenty years or so, that lacrosse finally took hold as a big-time sport in the United States and Canada.

Today, lacrosse is so popular that it just may be the fastest growing sport in America.

Lacrosse is a fusion of several other sports. It combines aspects of popular games like basketball, soccer, and hockey and rolls everything together into one exciting sport. The game is fast-paced, and action moves around the playing field with lightning quickness. Players sprint up and down the field as fast as they can, hoping to score a goal by using their sticks to flick the ball into the opponent's net. The opposing team tries desperately to keep this from happening. Possession of the ball constantly changes as each team struggles to gain momentum.

Lacrosse requires an immense amount of teamwork. Passing the ball between players is fundamental—without passing and cooperation among teammates, it would be impossible to win. Lacrosse also requires commitment. It takes a lot of effort and practice to become good at the game and years of play before skills can be mastered. Lacrosse rarely comes easy—even for the best of players. If lacrosse is your game, you'd better be willing to work.

So what does it take to be a lacrosse player? First, you need to want to play the game. Like any other sport, a passion for lacrosse will make you a better player. Once you get going, it helps to be quick on your feet. Fast runners are rewarded with goals. It also helps to be nimble with your hands—good hand-eye coordination can be the key to scooping, catching, passing, and handling the ball. You have to be in good shape, of course, but that will come once you start playing. The most important thing you need is a good attitude. With the right mind-set, anyone can succeed at lacrosse. Just get out and play!

If lacrosse is the oldest sport in North America, you might guess it has a great history. And you'd be right. Lacrosse has been passed down through the years from generation to generation ever since Native Americans invented an early form of the game back in the fifteenth century. From those early beginnings, lacrosse developed and evolved into the sport we know today—a sport played and loved by thousands and enjoyed by both men and women, from grade school children to college athletes to professionals.

In the Beginning . . .

Lacrosse was created by the many Native American tribes of eastern North America in the fifteenth century. It was then, and perhaps even earlier (it is impossible to know for certain), that Native Americans began playing a game using sticks, a ball, and some sort of designated goal. Games were played on fields, but the fields used by Native Americans centuries ago were nothing like the fields of today. There were no boundaries. There was no referee. There was only one major rule: no hands. However, over the centuries, the objective of the game has remained the same: put the ball in the other team's goal.

Instead of using their hands, the Native Americans who played this early version of lacrosse used sticks. Southeastern tribes (including the Cherokee) used two short sticks to pin and carry a ball made from deer-skin. Northern tribes located in the Great Lakes region took a slightly different approach. They used a single 3-foot-long (0.9-meter-long)

Lacrosse—America's Hottest Sport?

According to U.S. Lacrosse, the main organizing body for lacrosse played in the United States, lacrosse is currently one of the hottest games in town. Consider these facts:

- An estimated 250,000 men, women, and children play lacrosse in the United States.
- The number of lacrosse players nationwide is increasing at a rate of 20 percent each year.

- More than 72,000 boys and 15,000 girls play high school lacrosse.
- More than 25,000 men and 5,500 women play college lacrosse.
- At least 125,000 kids ages five to fifteen play organized lacrosse through youth and recreation programs.
- There are more than 300 lacrosse camps for boys and girls throughout the United States.

Every year, the official rules for girls' youth lacrosse are published in U.S. Lacrosse's women's rules book. U.S. Lacrosse's rules for girls include information on what equipment to use and on the many playing positions.

Lacrosse is North America's oldest sport. Native Americans had been playing their version of lacrosse for hundreds of years before the Europeans arrived. The Native Americans played the sport for religious reasons but mainly for the honor of their tribes.

stick with one end carved into a spoonlike scoop. They used the scoop to pick up, carry, and throw the ball. Still other tribes, especially those in the Northeast (like the Iroquois), played the game with longer sticks attached. They fastened webbing to the end of the stick and formed it into a small pocket in which the ball could be held.

The game, played primarily by male warriors, was typically played for fun, as a sort of practice to make fighters tougher and stronger. But the game was also used to settle arguments between tribes. If two tribes disagreed on tribal boundaries or who could claim which hunting grounds, they would sometimes go to battle not with knives and arrows but with sticks and ball.

Before each game began, religious ceremonies were often held to honor the players and acknowledge the spirits that were believed to oversee the tribes. Between 100 and 1,000 warriors at a time would play from sunrise to sunset, and games could last for days. Goalposts were usually made of two poles, trees, large rocks, or some other objects that would mark the goal. Some of these goalposts were miles apart from each other, creating an enormous goal. The ball was made of anything the Native Americans could find—typically wood, rock, hardened clay, or animal hide. (Today, lacrosse balls are made of hard rubber and are about the size of a tennis ball.) Additionally, the playing field had no boundaries.

The players ran far and wide across the countryside, dodging trees and rocks and jumping streams and rivers. They would carry the ball as far as they could before they were overtaken by an opponent or before they became exhausted. At that point, they would toss the ball to a teammate, who would then continue to run as far as he could go before passing, scoring, or losing possession of the ball to an opponent. Not surprisingly, considering the stakes involved, the game was often rough and violent. Many players were hurt. Some were even killed while playing.

A New Kind of Game

By the seventeenth century, the Native American game had attracted spectators. The first European settlers were spellbound by this strange

To the Native Americans, lacrosse was a festive and colorful game. These two paintings depict tribal warriors wearing what was common during lacrosse matches. Their attire most likely represented their tribes, much like an early version of a uniform.

and exciting new game. These Europeans were Jesuit missionaries who had come to America from France to spread their beliefs about God. They had never seen anything like this sport played by the Native Americans. The Europeans were fascinated by the athleticism and bravery of the players, as well as by the speed at which the game was played. Most intriguing to them, however, was the equipment. The Jesuit missionaries thought the type of stick used by the Native Americans looked a lot like a *crosse*, the French word for the staff carried by Catholic bishops during religious ceremonies. Eventually, they began referring to the game itself as *la crosse* ("the crosse"), and the name stuck.

Before long, settlers went from passive observers of the game to active participants. The first non–Native Americans to play lacrosse were probably Canadians from Montreal in the early 1800s. As the Canadians learned the sport from Native American tribes, they applied new rules and regulations they felt were necessary to keep things "civilized." They weren't comfortable with the freewheeling nature of the game—things like the lack of boundaries, the random goals, and the unlimited number of players allowed to participate at any one time. By the mid-1800s, a Montreal dentist named W. George Beers was at the forefront of a movement to organize lacrosse and introduce the sport to the rest of Canada.

Beers and others helped lacrosse to grow quickly in popularity among Canadians. Lacrosse clubs were created, and games were organized and played before spectators. Official rules were established, the number of players was standardized, and permanent goals were created. Eventually, the game became so popular that it was declared Canada's national sport. Soon the sport spread south to the United States and east to Europe as Canadians traveled to other countries to play exhibition games and show off "their" sport. All the while Native Americans continued to play their original form of the game.

Organized Lacrosse

In the nineteenth century, modern lacrosse began to evolve from the Canadian game. In the United States, eastern cities and schools established clubs and teams. In 1877, New York University became the

Over the years, lacrosse was adapted by European Americans. In the late nineteenth century, lacrosse developed into a more organized sport and began to spread to other countries. This photo captures the action of early organized women's lacrosse in England.

first American college to field a lacrosse team. A few years later, preparatory high schools followed suit. Phillips Academy Andover in Massachusetts, Phillips Exeter Academy in New Hampshire, and the Lawrenceville School in New Jersey all established lacrosse programs for their students in 1882.

As the game caught on, more and more teams were formed. Rivalries soon emerged between high schools and colleges. Clubs

By the early twentieth century, lacrosse was very popular in colleges in the eastern United States, Canada, and parts of Europe. Here, two players representing Canada and England fight for the ball during a game in 1905.

from various cities traveled long distances to play foes from other states or across the border in Canada. Women's teams were formed in the 1890s. By the early twentieth century, the game had become so popular that the players and others who loved the game decided to create an organizing body to oversee the sport's development. Before long, the United States Intercollegiate Lacrosse League (USILL) was established. The international community got its first taste of lacrosse when the game appeared as an exhibition sport in the 1904 Olympics in St. Louis, Missouri. The USILL continued to act as the governing body for lacrosse in the United States until it was replaced by the United States Intercollegiate Lacrosse Association (USILA) in 1926.

The Modern Sport

Today, as rules have been ironed out and equipment has become standardized, men's and women's lacrosse are similar, but in many respects they have gone their separate ways. The women's game remains somewhat true to the game Native Americans played centuries ago. Little protective equipment is used in the women's game because body contact is not allowed and stick contact is limited. Women also continue to use wooden sticks. Men, on the other hand, can "check" each other like they do in hockey, using their bodies and sticks to gain position and force opponents out of the way. The men use high-tech and lightweight aluminum, titanium, and plastic sticks. Helmets and padding are also worn for protection in the men's game.

The modern game is steadily growing in popularity, with thousands of lacrosse teams both nationwide and worldwide. In the United States alone, an estimated 250,000 people play lacrosse. Now hundreds of high schools and colleges, both private and public, field lacrosse teams—a huge leap from the half-dozen or so that pioneered the sport back in the 1800s. Tens of thousands of spectators attend collegiate lacrosse championships each year, flocking in droves to watch young athletes battle for top honors in their respective divisions.

Lacrosse has developed immensely over the past century. Additionally, the popularity of the sport has spread across the globe. More and more schools and organizations are springing up every year to offer organized lacrosse to men and women of all ages.

Today, although lacrosse continues to be a mostly amateur sport, there are two professional leagues in the United States. The National Lacrosse League (NLL) oversees the indoor teams, while Major League Lacrosse (MLL) administers the outdoor league. National teams have also been established in dozens of countries, and world championships are held each year to determine which team will be named the best on the planet.

CHAPTER TWO

On the Field

A good lacrosse game is filled with action and fast-moving players. Sprints up and down the field, sudden starts and stops, precision passes, and dodges are standard parts of this game.

Like any team sport, lacrosse requires players to work together in order to win. The objective in lacrosse is clear: score a goal by putting the ball into the opponent's net. The team with the most goals at the end of the game wins. It's not that easy, of course, as there are a few rules and regulations that players must follow, with slight differences between the men's game and the women's game. There are also numerous set plays in lacrosse—the type of plays you might witness in a game of football, for example. Players make special, choreographed moves with or without the ball in an effort to get open to receive a pass, to help a teammate get open, or to get off a shot at the opponent's goal. Lacrosse is a complicated game. The basics, however, are easy to learn.

Positions

In men's lacrosse, there are four major positions on the lacrosse field: attack, midfield, defense, and goal. The men's lacrosse team consists of three attackmen, three midfielders, three defenders, and one goalie. In all, ten players take the field at a time for each team, while substitutes wait on the sidelines to relieve those who get tired or hurt. The women's game includes twelve players per team: six attackers and six defenders. The attack positions include center, right, and left attack wings; third home; second home; and first home. The defenders include right and left defense wings, third man, cover point, point, and goalie. The women's game also allows for substitutes that can come in off the bench during the game.

The job of people who play attack is to score. Attackmen, as these players are called, must stay on the offensive side of the field—that is, the side of the field with their opponent's goal. Attackmen possess excellent stick-handling skills so they can make accurate shots and passes. They are also usually the quickest and most agile players on the team so they can make moves around defenders on their way to the goal.

Each position on a lacrosse team has its own important role in the game. Here, the offensive players *(dark jerseys)* move the ball into their opponent's scoring zone. Defenders *(light jerseys)* move in to slow their progress or to gain control of the ball.

Here, the attacker *(light jersey)* cradles the ball while trying to make a pass or shoot. The defender *(dark jersey)* tries to keep the attacker out of shooting or passing range. The defender carries a longer and thicker stick to aid defense of his or her goal.

This goalkeeper is getting ready to make a save. The goalie is the last means of defense from keeping the opposing team from scoring. The goalkeeper carries a stick with a larger net to help catch or block the ball more effectively.

Attackmen practice things like setting picks for teammates. A pick is a strategic move where one player stands still or moves slowly as another player with the ball runs around him or her. The ballcarrier uses the pick as a shield for protection against defenders. The attackmen work together with each other and the midfielders to move the ball around the goal until a hole in the defense opens up and they can get off a shot.

The men's game has an additional position called midfielder. Midfielders are the only players that can roam the entire field. They play both offense and defense and act as the connection between defense and offense, moving the ball away from their net toward their opponent's. Midfielders must be adept at scoring like the attackmen, but they also must have the defensive skills of the defenders. The midfielders almost always do the most running during a lacrosse game because they have the most ground to cover.

Defenders have the honor of defending their own goal and must stay on their own side of the field. In the men's game, the three defenders carry 6-foot-long (1.8-meter-long) sticks that they use to try to knock the ball out of the hands of the opposing team's attackers and midfielders. They try to stop or disrupt any offensive charge and try to gain control of the ball and send it into their opponent's side.

The last player on the team, and perhaps the most important, is the goalie. The goalie's job is to prevent the other team from scoring by being the last line of defense before the goal. Wearing extra padding, the goalie must be both fast and fearless, using the stick to stop the shots of the opposition. The goalie also often acts as the first player to set the offense in motion. After stopping a shot, the goalie passes the ball out to a running teammate, who can then move the ball upfield to begin the attack on the other goal.

How the Game Is Played

High school lacrosse games are generally forty-eight minutes long and divided into four quarters of twelve minutes each. In college, the games are sixty minutes long with four fifteen-minute quarters. Players are given short breaks between each quarter and a slightly longer break between the first and second halves of the game. Youth games are often shorter than the high school matches.

Teams are typically permitted three time-outs per game, with a maximum of two time-outs in any one half. The teams change sides of the field after each quarter to prevent either team from gaining an unfair advantage from field or weather conditions.

In the men's game, field boundaries are marked by lines painted on the ground. In addition, a so-called crease surrounds the goal to protect the goalie and give him room to maneuver. This crease is circular in shape and 18 feet (5.5 meters) in diameter. Only the goalie and his teammates are allowed to enter the crease area. However, opposing players can reach in with their sticks to try to get the ball.

Other field marks include a midfield line, found exactly halfway between the two goals, as well as lines denoting wing areas and restraining areas. The wing areas mark the spots on either side of center field where the outside midfielders must wait until the whistle is blown at face-off. The offensive and defensive restraining areas are the spots where the three attackmen and three defenders and goalie must

The differences between men's and women's lacrosse playing fields are not the only differences in the game. The rules for men's lacrosse allow physical contact between the players, while the women's rules do not. The men's game is played by ten players per team, while women's lacrosse is played by twelve players per team.

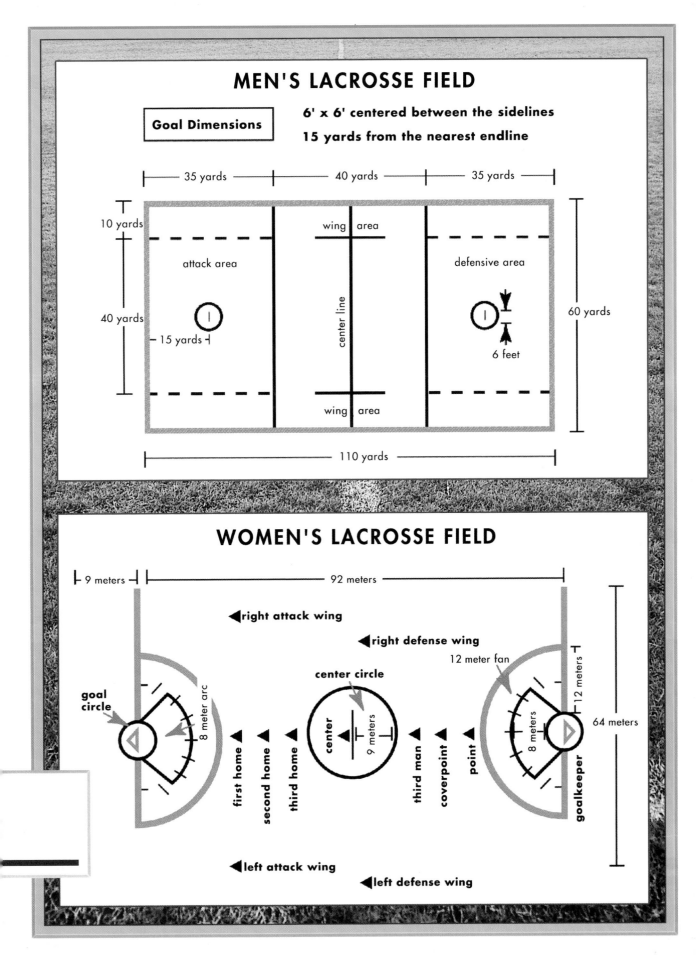

MEN'S LACROSSE FIELD

Goal Dimensions

6' x 6' centered between the sidelines
15 yards from the nearest endline

35 yards — 40 yards — 35 yards

10 yards

wing area

attack area

defensive area

center line

40 yards

15 yards

6 feet

60 yards

wing area

110 yards

WOMEN'S LACROSSE FIELD

9 meters

92 meters

right attack wing

right defense wing

12 meter fan

center circle

goal circle

8 meter arc

center

9 meters

12 meters

8 meters

8 meters

64 meters

first home
second home
third home

third man
coverpoint
point

goalkeeper

left attack wing

left defense wing

wait until one of the midfielders has possession of the ball following the face-off. Once a midfielder gains possession of the ball, the other players can rush in and join the action.

The women's lacrosse field has no boundaries. There are no lines marking the outer limits of the field and preventing players from running as far as they want. Certain markings do exist, however, around the goal and at center field. Unlike the men's game, there is no midfield line that divides the field into two equal halves. There is also a crease around the goal in which only the goalie and her defensive teammates are allowed to enter. An arc, in the shape of a half-circle, is also painted around the goal, but it comes out farther than the crease. This arc is the line players must stay behind during a penalty shot.

The Whistle Blows

The game starts with a face-off at the center of the field. An *X* on the field marks the spot. In the men's game, two players crouch down on either side of the *X*. They place their sticks on the ground with the backs of the sticks facing each other. The referee places the ball between the two sticks while the other players stand to the side in the restraining areas or, in the case of the midfielders, in the wing areas. When the referee blows the whistle, the match begins. The two players at the face-off use their sticks to fight for possession of the ball, trying to scoop the ball off the ground as quickly as possible. Meanwhile, the wing midfielders sprint in to help out. Once possession is gained by either team, the other players are released from their restraining areas and the game swings into full motion. The team with the ball begins to move toward their opponent's goal upfield, and the team without the ball defends.

A face-off always starts off the men's game. Two opposing attackers meet at the center of the field. The game ball is placed in front of them, between their sticks, as both players crouch down. The whistle blows, and the two attackers wrestle to gain possession of the ball for their team.

The women's game kicks off differently from the men's game. Two players at the center of the field begin with the backs of their sticks pressed together and the ball held tightly between. The other players stand outside of a large center circle and wait for the referee's signal. When the whistle blows, the two centers push their sticks together as hard as they can as they try to cause their opponent to drop the ball. Meanwhile, the other players from each team rush in from the edge of the circle. Typically, the ball pops high up into the air and players jump and reach with their sticks to catch it and gain possession.

Game On

With a team finally in possession of the ball, the game starts rolling. Players cradle the ball in the webbing at the end of their sticks by using the force generated by a rapid back-and-forth curling motion of the wrists. This keeps the ball glued to the stick's net even while the players move quickly downfield. The player with the ball runs as far as he or she wants or passes the ball to a teammate who might be open and in better position to move the ball toward the opponent's goal. The player with the ball must, however, be aware of the opposition at all times. The opposing players will do everything they can to steal or knock the ball away. The only way to move the ball is with the stick, as hands can be used by only one player—the goalie.

If the ball goes out of bounds, play stops. In the case of the women's game, play stops when the referee blows the whistle because the ball has gone somewhere he or she deems to be dangerous or too far away. In the men's game, when a ball goes out of bounds or if a player steps out of bounds while carrying the ball, play stops and the other team is awarded possession of the ball. In the women's game, whoever has the ball (or is closest to the ball) when the referee blows the whistle keeps possession. The player must then bring the ball back toward the goals. If a ball goes out of bounds following a shot, whoever is closest to the ball gets possession.

As players duck and weave their way downfield toward the opposing goal, they must take special care to avoid losing possession of the ball to the other team's defenders. Defenders have many ways

The attacker *(white jersey)* cradles the ball toward the goal while the defender *(dark jersey)* sprints to block passes or shots on goal. Here, the defender looks to check the ball from the attacker's stick and knock the ball away to stop or slow the attack.

they can take the ball from a player. They can use their sticks to poke, or "stick check," the ballcarrier's gloves and stick in an effort to knock the ball away. In the men's game, they can also hit the ballcarrier with their bodies, delivering a body check in much the same way hockey players do. For safety reasons, these checks must be delivered to the front or side of the player and kept above the waist and below the shoulders. The women's game does not allow body contact between players. Stick checks, which are allowed in both games, can also be delivered to any player in an effort to keep him or her from gaining possession while a loose ball is in the air or on the ground.

The Goal

In high school and college games, the lacrosse goal is 6 feet (1.8 meters) tall and 6 feet (1.8 m) wide. Youth leagues often play with smaller goals to make it easier for smaller goalies to defend.

As the offense moves the ball toward the opposing goal, they look for an open shot. If they get one off, the goalie tries to catch or block the ball from going into the goal. The goalie uses the huge basket on his or her stick or uses his or her body to stop the ball in the air. Once the goalie has possession of the ball in the crease area, he or she must be left alone and cannot be checked in any fashion. The "keeper," as the goalie is known, then has four seconds to either pass the ball to a teammate or leave the crease area and move onto the open field. If the goalie holds the ball for more than four seconds within the crease, or if he or she steps out of the crease and then steps back in, the ball is turned over to the other team. If the offense is lucky enough to score a goal, the referee takes the ball and moves it back to the center of the field for another face-off.

Rules and Regulations

To keep the game from getting out of control, personal fouls may be called and penalties administered by referees in response to inappropriate actions by players. When a foul is committed, the offending player can be suspended from play for anywhere from one to three

The lacrosse goal has a square frame with three sides covered in netting. Here, the goalie poises to receive a shot on goal. Defenders rush in to stop attackers from interfering with the goalie's save.

minutes, depending on the severity of the foul. If a referee calls five fouls on any one player, that player must leave the game for good.

Fouls include slashing, tripping, cross-checking, unsportsmanlike conduct, unnecessary roughness, and illegal checking. Slashing is called when a player hacks at an opponent with his or her stick and hits the person anywhere other than on the hands or stick. Cross-checking occurs when a player checks an opponent using the handle of his or her

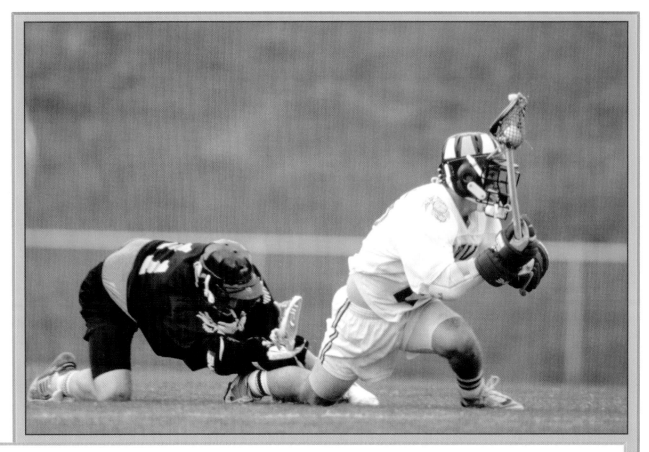

Lacrosse can be very physical and dangerous. Here, a defender *(left)* takes down an offensive player with an illegal move. Penalties are common and occur throughout the game. Like any other sport, practice, physical conditioning, and fair play can greatly reduce the amount of injuries from lacrosse.

stick instead of his or her body. Unsportsmanlike conduct is exactly what it sounds like: swearing, making insults, and arguing with an official all qualify. Unnecessary roughness may be called if a player uses excessive force or violence on an opponent. Illegal body checking occurs when a player checks an opponent who doesn't have the ball or isn't within 5 yards (4.6 m) of a loose ball. It can also be called if a player intentionally checks someone after he or she has passed or shot the ball, if a check is given below the waist, from behind, or above the shoulders, or if both hands are not on the stick when the check is delivered.

Penalties can also be given for using illegal equipment. Not all lacrosse sticks, for instance, are legal. If the pocket is too deep or the stick is altered to make it more effective for ballhandling or shooting, the player can receive a penalty. Gloves, too, can be illegal if they have been altered by the player to make it easier to handle the stick.

Technical fouls can be called for things like holding, interference, pushing from behind, or stalling. Most of these infractions are self-explanatory. Offsides is another penalty. It occurs when a team has fewer than four players on the defensive half of the field or fewer than three players on the offensive side. The offsides rule is meant to keep balance on the field, so all the players don't stock up on the offensive or defensive side of the field. Screening, another penalty, is called when a player blocks an opponent and prevents him or her from guarding someone else. Warding off is a common foul called when a player with the ball uses his or her non-stick-carrying hand to block the stick checks of an opponent. Unlike the more severe penalties for personal fouls, these technical fouls result in a mere thirty-second player suspension and transfer of possession to the other team.

There are lots of other rules and regulations, with variations between the men's game and the women's game, between indoor lacrosse and outdoor lacrosse, and between youth leagues and adult leagues that are easily picked up on the field. The best way to learn all about these rules and regulations and make them second nature is to get out and play!

CHAPTER THREE

The Competitive Spirit

Cooperation and respect are crucial skills in lacrosse today. In its early days, however, the game was also a way for men to prepare for war.

One of the best things about lacrosse is how quickly it is growing in popularity. Youth lacrosse leagues are sprouting up all over the country. Meanwhile, local and regional tournaments are becoming more and more common. Indoor lacrosse—a slightly different version of the game played indoors on either artificial turf or in a gym—can be played all winter long in colder climates. Outdoor lacrosse—typically played on grass—is the choice for those who play in the warmer months. Girls and boys play together in some youth leagues, while in other leagues they have their own teams. Take a look around. Lacrosse is almost everywhere!

College Lacrosse

Many high school standouts go on to play lacrosse in college, whether for clubs or varsity teams. Although both club and varsity teams may represent a school, club teams support themselves through player fees, fund-raising, and tournament fees. Varsity teams enjoy financial support provided by their school. These teams compete with other schools in the region or across the country, depending on the league. The National Collegiate Athletic Association (NCAA) includes dozens of men's and women's lacrosse teams that compete each year for the NCAA championship. Schools like Johns Hopkins University in Maryland and Syracuse University in New York are two of the better-known universities with top lacrosse programs.

Many colleges also sponsor intramural leagues. These leagues are for lacrosse players who may not be interested in playing lacrosse at a highly competitive college level but still wish to play just for the fun of it. Intramural leagues are a great way to stay in shape, play with friends, or rekindle a love for the game. Intramural teams all come from the same college—that is, one college might have ten intramural teams that play each other during the intramural season. At the end of the season, one of those teams is crowned the intramural champion for the college.

Professional Lacrosse

Very few lacrosse players ever play competitively beyond the collegiate level. There are local clubs and leagues for adults, of course, but these leagues are typically not at the same competitive level as collegiate lacrosse. For players who are outstanding in college, however, there is one option: professional lacrosse.

Professional lacrosse, where the players are actually paid to play the game they love, is a relatively new phenomenon in the United States. The National Lacrosse League (NLL), formed in 1986, is the men's professional indoor lacrosse league in the United States. Also known as box lacrosse, indoor lacrosse comes with an entirely different set of rules from that of outdoor lacrosse. It is a bit more like ice hockey, where the action takes place inside an enclosed arena. Therefore, indoor lacrosse is extremely fast and is highly physical. Currently, there are fourteen teams on the indoor circuit, and the season runs from January to April. Games typically attract between 5,000 and 15,000 fans.

Professional men's outdoor (field) lacrosse is organized by Major League Lacrosse (MLL). Established in 2001, MLL today has just six teams, all based on the East Coast: the Baltimore Bayhawks, Boston Cannons, Philadelphia Barrage, Long Island (NY) Lizards, New Jersey Pride, and Rochester (NY) Rattlers. Players, many of whom also play in the indoor league, endure thirty-six regular-season matches from

The popularity of lacrosse has reached the professional level. The United States boasts two professional lacrosse leagues: the NLL and MLL. The NLL is indoor lacrosse with a season that runs from early winter through late spring. MLL is outdoor lacrosse with a season that runs through the summer.

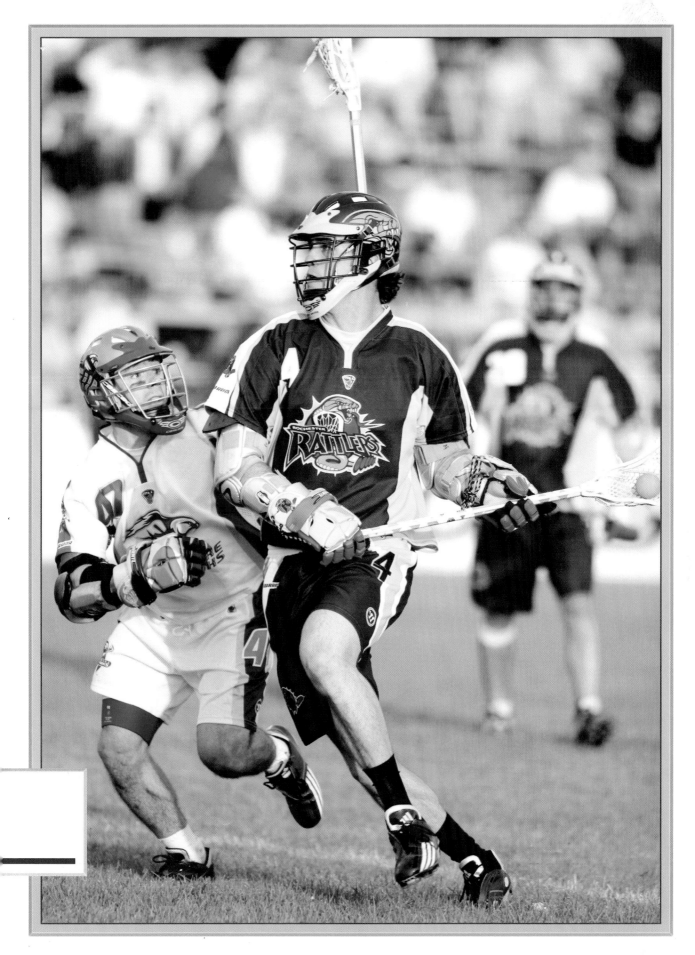

June through September. The best players also take part in an all-star game, an event designed to showcase the skills of the top players in the world. At the end of each season, a tournament is held to determine the league champion.

World Lacrosse

Beyond the professional leagues in North America, there is one last level of competition—world lacrosse. Teams from all over the planet, including Europe, Asia, and elsewhere, gather each year to play against each other and proudly represent their respective countries. These players are the best of the best. They play lacrosse like no one else can.

Every four years, the Men's Lacrosse World Championship is held by the International Lacrosse Federation (ILF), the governing body of international lacrosse competition. The United States has done extremely well in this tournament, winning the title every year but one since the competition began in the early 1970s in Melbourne, Australia. The United States' only loss came against Canada in 1978. Most recently, the United States beat Canada for the 2002 title in Perth, Australia.

This dominance says a lot about the U.S. athletes and their devotion to the game. It also says something about the state of lacrosse in the United States. Perhaps the United States' mastery of the game is due to the abundance of youth leagues,. Here, kids can start the game at a young age, learning to master important skills almost as soon as they begin to walk. Or maybe it's the fact that so many high schools now have lacrosse programs, where kids can continue to hone their skills as the competitive level increases. It could be the incredible collegiate lacrosse competition and all the quality players it produces.

The Gait Brothers: Lacrosse Superstars

Few players, if any, have made as big an impact on the game of lacrosse as two brothers from Canada: Paul and Gary Gait. Their accomplishments on the field have led to the brothers being known as a sibling version of hockey's Wayne Gretzky and basketball's Michael Jordan. The Gait brothers have won almost every lacrosse honor there is to win. They've revolutionized the game like no one before them. The Gait brothers have been, hands down, the most dominant lacrosse players in the history of the sport.

The Gait brothers first came on the national scene as college players at Syracuse University in New York. Playing a game in which they seemed to score at will, the two dominated college play, leading the Syracuse Orangemen to three NCAA Division I championships. They both went on to play professionally, and both set numerous records. The Gait brothers currently share the record for most goals scored in an NLL game with ten apiece.

It's impossible to even begin to describe the many ways in which the Gait brothers have left their stamp on the game. But consider these words, as published in the *Calgary Sun* newspaper, from Calgary Roughneck coach Chris Hall, who had the honor of coaching the Gaits when they were teens in Canada: "Both Gary and Paul are the complete package in terms of the prototypical lacrosse player. They have size, athleticism, speed, strength, skill, and intelligence. They're just the whole package." As anyone who has seen the Gait brothers play can attest, these two are the real deal. No one else even comes close.

No one has dominated the game of lacrosse quite like the Gait brothers. Paul and Gary *(above)* Gait were teammates at Syracuse University.

International play has helped spread the popularity of lacrosse across the globe. Today, several countries field both men's and women's teams to participate in international competitions. Here, Team USA goalie Jim Mule blocks a shot from Team Canada during the 1999 World Cup of Lacrosse held in Baltimore, Maryland.

Whatever the case, U.S. lacrosse is on top of the world, and by the looks of the players coming down the pipeline, it will continue to be for a long time.

Meanwhile, the International Federation of Women's Lacrosse Association (IFWLA) sponsors the World Cup, first held in Nottingham, England, in 1982. In 2001, the most recent World Cup was held, with the United States beating host Australia for the

Much of the popularity of women's lacrosse here in the United States can be attributed to the amazing success of its international team. Here, Team USA celebrates a win to be crowned champions of the Women's Lacrosse World Cup in Tokyo in 1997. It was the fifth consecutive cup championship for the team.

championship. Both the ILF and IFWLA organize major international championships for players under nineteen years of age.

CHAPTER FOUR

Getting Started

Gloves

Helmet

Shoulder Pads

Stick

To get started in organized lacrosse, you will need to figure out what equipment is right for you. The right equipment can help improve your play and reduce the chance for injury.

So you think you'd like to give lacrosse a try? Getting started is easy. All you have to do is be motivated to learn a great new sport. Give it a try, and you'll be hooked.

One of the best ways to get going—or at least to get excited about the sport—is to watch a lacrosse game. Go to a local high school or college and watch one of their games. Or, if you live in a city with a professional team, go see the pros hit the field. You can also sometimes catch lacrosse games on cable television stations like ESPN. Check out the action and see how the game works. You're sure to find it exciting and be anxious to get started playing yourself.

Equipment

To play lacrosse, you must have the right equipment. Most equipment is required for safety reasons. In addition, most lacrosse equipment must meet specific standards to be allowed for use.

The main piece of equipment necessary in both the men's and women's game is the stick. Sticks must be a certain length according to the position the player holds (attackmen use shorter sticks than defenders, for instance). The women's crosse has a shallower pocket than the men's crosse does, and in most cases, women are required to use wooden sticks while men can use sticks made of aluminum or titanium if they choose. Visit a sporting goods store or contact a store that specializes in lacrosse equipment. Ask questions and find out which crosse is best for you.

In addition to the stick, women wear mouthguards and, in many leagues, goggles for eye protection. Most also wear cleats, a jersey, and shorts or a kilt as their uniform. Padded gloves may be worn, but they're not required. Due to the more physical nature of the men's game, men are required to wear a helmet with a face mask, padded gloves, arm and shoulder pads, and a protective cup.

Goalies wear more padding than other players because they must block the ball when it is shot at the net. Women goalies wear

Women's lacrosse is growing more popular every year. More and more high schools and colleges now have girls' and women's lacrosse teams. If your school does not, you can find a women's lacrosse camp where you can learn the basics of the game.

There's no shortage of lacrosse equipment available. While your town might not have a lacrosse equipment store, the Internet offers plenty of places to find the right equipment for you.

Lacrosse's rise in popularity is showing no signs of slowing down. Each year, younger and younger kids are taking up lacrosse. As this trend increases, competition at every level, from high school to professional, improves and draws more fans.

a helmet with a face mask and throat protector, padded gloves, and arm, chest, and leg pads. The men wear almost the same thing, minus the leg pads.

Lacrosse equipment can be found in sporting goods stores all over the country, as well as online through many different manufacturer Web sites. Used gear is also an option, since many people like to "hand down" their equipment as they grow out of it.

Get Out and Play!

Once you discover lacrosse is something you want to try, getting started is as easy as joining your local youth lacrosse league. Most youth leagues are not very competitive because it's just for fun and many of the players are just learning the game. If you find you really enjoy the sport, you can then try out for more competitive teams, like a school team or traveling team. These teams will require lots of practice and dedication, but the rewards will be plenty. Being part of a team will allow you to make great friends while learning the spirit of teamwork.

You might live in a place without a youth lacrosse league. If this is the case, you might have to travel to join a team. If traveling is not an option, however, you still might be able to play. You'll just have to be ambitious. Talk to an adult who is willing to help out and see if you can organize a youth team yourself. At the very least, you should be able to get a coach and a bunch of kids together once or twice a week to learn how to play the sport. Similar to basketball or ice hockey, lacrosse can start simply through pickup games with your friends in a local park. Just keep in mind as you play that lacrosse is not just about winning games. The most important thing is to have fun!

GLOSSARY

crease   A line that surrounds the goal and serves as a buffer zone between the goal and goalie and the offensive players.

crosse   The lacrosse stick.

exhibition game   A demonstration game, one that is held to introduce the game to an audience.

penalty shot   A free shot at the goal awarded to an offensive player who has been fouled by the defense.

personal foul   A foul committed by a player against another player, resulting in a penalty.

referee   An official who oversees the game to make sure rules are followed and teams play fairly.

restraining area   An area of the field on which certain players must wait at every face-off before joining play.

stick check   A defensive technique in which a player will poke his or her stick at the ballcarrier in an attempt to make the other player drop the ball.

technical foul   A nonpersonal foul called on a player or team as a result of technical infractions, resulting in a penalty.

time-out   A short period of rest called for by a team during a game.

FOR MORE INFORMATION

Canadian Lacrosse Association
2211 Riverside Drive, Suite B-4
Ottawa, ON K1H 7X5
Canada
http://www.lacrosse.ca

U.S. Lacrosse
113 West University Parkway
Baltimore, MD 21210
(410) 235-6882
http://www.lacrosse.org

Web Sites

Due to the changing nature of Internet links, the Rosen Publishing Group, Inc., has developed an online list of Web sites related to the subject of this book. This site is updated regularly. Please use this link to access the list:

http://www.rosenlinks.com/scc/lacr

FOR FURTHER READING

Hinkson, Jim. *Lacrosse for Dummies*. New York: John Wiley and
Sons, Inc., 2003.

Scott, Bob. *Lacrosse Technique and Tradition*. New York: Johns
Hopkins University Press, 1978.

Urick, David. *Lacrosse: Fundamentals for Winning*. New York: Sports
Illustrated, 1991.

BIBLIOGRAPHY

Canadian Lacrosse Association. "A Short History." Retrieved September 2003 (http://www.lacrosse.ca/history.html).

Canadian Lacrosse Association. "The Philosophy of Lacrosse." Retrieved September 2003 (http://www.lacrosse.ca/philosohy.html).

U.S. Lacrosse. "About Lacrosse." Retrieved September 2003 (http://www.lacrosse.org).

INDEX

About the Author

Chris Hayhurst is a freelance writer living in Colorado.

Photo Credits

Cover (left image) © Mark Goldman/Icon SMI; cover (group and field), pp. 3, 4, 15, 16, 18, 21 (background field), 23, 38 by Dallas Hoppestad; cover (right image), p. 40 (top) © Howard C. Smith/ Icon SMI; pp. 7, 27, 30, 36, 37 © AP/Wide World Photos; p. 8 © Bettmann/Corbis; p. 10 General Research Division, New York Public Library, Astor, Lenox, and Tilden Foundations; p. 12 © Hulton/ Archive/ Getty Images; p. 13 Chicago Historical Society; p. 21 (field diagrams) by Nelson Sá; p. 25 © Chuck Solomon/SI/Icon SMI; p. 28 © Paul A. Souders/Corbis; p. 33 © Jerome Davis/Icon SMI; p. 35 Bill Vaughan/Icon SMI; p. 40 (middle) © Lacrosse.com; p. 40 (bottom) © Bob Falcetti/Icon SMI.

The Rosen Publishing Group, Inc., would like to thank St. Andrew's Episcopal School in Austin, Texas, for the use of its lacrosse field in this project.

Designer: Nelson Sá; **Editor:** Charles Hofer;
Photo Researcher: Sherri Liberman